Staying Steady in Unsteady Times

by
Tim Storey

Harrison House
Tulsa, Oklahoma

06   10 9 8 7 6 5 4 3

Staying Steady in Unsteady Times
ISBN-13: 978-1-57794-587-1
ISBN-10: 1-57794-587-5
Copyright © 2003 by Tim Storey
P.O. Box 1428
Whittier, California 90609

Published by Harrison House, Inc.
P.O. Box 35035
Tulsa, Oklahoma 74153

Printed in the United States of America. All rights reserved under International Copyright Law. Contents and/or cover may not be reproduced in whole or in part in any form without the express written consent of the Publisher.

Contents

Introduction

Sometimes life gets unsteady. That's just a fact, and there's no escaping it. Maybe you've suffered so much pain and trauma that you've given up on ever seeing solid ground again. Maybe you haven't laughed in a long time. Maybe you've been laid off, stabbed in the back by a friend or family member, robbed, beaten, abandoned, rejected, or abused, so you're angry and ready to quit.

I know where you're coming from. Do you know how many times I wanted to quit, to just sit back and wallow in self-pity because I was tired of all the cheap shots and battles? But I didn't give up, and I didn't stay unsteady. And you can't either. I'll tell you why, but you have to picture this.

I'm walking through the Dallas-Fort Worth Airport so tired my feet are dragging ten steps behind me. This great motivator isn't feeling good at all. My hair's all whacked out. I've got my hat pulled down as far as it will go and my dark glasses on. I'm walking with my head down so I don't have to see or talk to anybody. I'm in one of those "don't mess with me" moods. That's right: Even "Mr. Encourager" has that kind of day—not often, but I'm being real with you and it does happen sometimes. It takes a lot to get me that way because I am up 98 percent of the time, but I was *down* that day.

A little lady comes running up to me, calling, "Tim Storey, Tim Storey, Tim...." I'm thinking, "Oh no. Not today." So I say, "Yeah?"

She says, "I don't want to bother you, but...." Then she proceeds to share a remarkable story: "You were at a church in Baton Rouge, Louisiana, and the place was packed to the rafters—over 6,500 people. I was sitting in the second row, too weak to come forward, but your message and prayers became my light at the end of the tunnel when I was dying of cancer. Tim, that was three years ago. They gave me three weeks to live, and I'm not dead!"

What I want you to hear from this story is that in the middle of unsteady times, people need hope. I don't care how far you think you've sunk into the pit of despair, how desperately you've failed, how tragic your circumstances are, or how badly you're hurting. Even if the solid ground of life has suddenly started shaking, splitting, and sinking around you, stay steady: God has already prepared your breakthrough, and your testimony is waiting to be told.

Chapter 1

When Life Gets Unsteady

My father died when I was ten, a tough age for a boy to lose his dad. Three years later a call came that my sister had been in a terrible car accident. We went to Modesto, California, to pray for her. She was in a coma for eight days and then died. Everybody in the family was having a hard time. Some were tripping up big time, but I watched my mother as she kept believing, kept trusting, kept holding on to the promises of God. She taught me by example what it means to stay steady in unsteady times.

Life isn't perfect, and that is a fact we must accept. We live in a world where the enemy is alive and well. He isn't going to allow God's purposes to be fulfilled in His people without putting up a fight, so we've got to learn to hold on to God's hand and stay steady—especially when life seems most unsteady.

No matter how much debris is flying in your face from the storms of life right now, this isn't the time to give up. During the terrible storms created by El Niño in 1998, a devastating tornado hit a Southern community. A third-grader and her classmates huddled in the school hallway as the funnel cloud roared overhead. In a tv news interview, when the girl was asked if she was afraid, she replied matter-of-factly, "No. I just cried and prayed to Jesus." No one at the school was injured. What an awesome testimony of what it means to stay steady during unsteady times!

Like this young girl, you have to stay steady in faith for the peaceful time ahead. Even if you have to pray through tears, don't get discouraged. You aren't alone, and you aren't the first person to go through an unsteady time. Look at what others before you have done.

Remember, for instance, all Abraham had to go through before Isaac was born. (Genesis 12-21.) God did the impossible by giving a 100-year-old couple a child, but it didn't happen without numerous challenges, even after God had spoken the promise to Abraham and Sarah.

Like them, you will have to fight to obtain the promise God gives you. Opposition is going to come, so expect it and deal with it. Just determine to be steady so you can do the big things God has in mind for you.

Remember, also, that when God revealed the Promised Land to Joshua and Caleb, they had to climb mountains and confront giants that opposed and challenged their right to possess the promise. You can be sure that there will be mountains in the way and giants on top of every one of your promises. Those mountains and giants want nothing less than to knock you off your course toward the promise.

They're like the waves in the ocean when you're surfing. I remember surfing in Hawaii once: Picture me with this big Afro, bodysurfing with all the locals. The waves were big, and I wasn't used to the currents and undertow. A wave would hit and knock me down. I'd try to get up, and another wave would come and hit me—again and again and again. Finally, it pulled my swimsuit clean off me. I had to swim around and find my swimsuit before I could go to shore, all the while still being hit with those big waves.

Life seems that way sometimes, doesn't it? You get hit and get back up. *Bam!* You get hit again. *Bam!* Something else hits. Knocks your drawers off! Now you've got to chase down your drawers while the waves keep hitting. You feel like saying, "Stop already! Just leave me alone! I don't want to change. I like 'me' just the way I am." But you're not a person who is just going to barely get by. You're a trailblazer, a world shaker, and a history maker. You'll encounter obstacles and opposition and the discomfort of unsteady times, but you're coming out of it all a changed person!

Even while you're feeling the sting of this recent unexpected blow in your life—the sting of "I can't believe I have cancer," the sting of "I can't believe he left me," the sting of "I should have gotten that job"—there's a breakthrough plan already being orchestrated. God is getting you ready, preparing you for your victory right now. If you are plugged in to God, He is creating somebody different inside of you, making you into the person He wants you to be.

So when the waves, the mountains, and the giants pop up on your way to God's promise, don't let them steal your hope and expectation. Against all hope, against all challenges, against all waves, against all mountains, against all giants, you've got to believe in hope. God is hope, and He is able to do all things. Didn't He say to Abraham and Sarah, "Is anything too hard for Me?" (Genesis 18:14.)

That same Almighty God the Father—Your Daddy—is a winner. And you were made in His image. So guess what. You were born to win. So when you find yourself in an unsteady time, remember: *It's only temporary.* God hasn't brought you this far to leave you.

All the promises of God for you are yea and amen. That's why your life is going to have a happy ending, whether you believe it or not right now. You're the head and not the tail. You're above and not beneath. You're going over and not under. And no weapon formed against you shall prosper! You're going to be all right because God is on your side!

Chapter 2

❦

Hold on to the Promise

Before your God-appointed ascension (your victory) takes place, the enemy's attempted assassination (an unsteady time) will try to prevent it. You may be one step from your breakthrough when all hell breaks loose.

When I was a little kid chasing the ice cream truck, flying my kite, and beating up my neighbors, I never knew life could take so many strange turns. Everything would be going great. Then all of a sudden *bam*, along came a turn of events that didn't just rock the boat; it deployed a depth charge. When I was knocked down further than I'd ever known I could get, all I had to go on was God's promise that He'd turn everything around and use me to do things I'd never even dreamed of.

According to *Webster's Dictionary*, a promise is a vow that provides a basis or reason for expectation of success, improvement, or excellence.[1] It is a reason for hope. When God gives you a promise, it pumps you up and you say, "Yes! I can do it." Once you get the "Yes, I can" spirit down in your heart, you're on the home stretch to your victory.

But first, you may have to flex your faith muscles to keep holding on to the promise when resistance comes. I can remember in sixth grade we had to do the President's Physical Fitness Test. One guy in class we called "Little Ricky" wasn't little at all, and he had a hard time doing even one pull-up. But we loved Ricky because he was funny, so when the teacher wasn't looking we'd help him up: "One...two...three...." We'd say,

---

[1] Webster, Vol. 2, p. 1166.

"Hey, look at little Ricky! Ohhh! That boy can do some pull-ups!" We'd help him out so he'd do okay on his test. But as he struggled with each pull-up, he started saying, "I'm gonna...I'm gonna...I'm gonna do...I'm gonna do some of them things...I'm gonna lose some weight." Sure enough, by eighth grade Ricky was doing pull-ups—swoosh, swoosh, swoosh. He caught the "Yes, I can" spirit and held on to his promise.

I caught that spirit when I was in Bible college. Some friends and I hopped into my Honda Civic and drove four hours to go see a man named Paul [David] Yongii Cho, a man who'd had tuberculosis as a teenager, was healed, and believed God for a great church in Seoul, Korea. This man stood at the podium and in broken English said, "You must believe the Lord; you must visualize what the Lord can do."

Preaching on great faith, he said, "There are measures of faith. You can grow your faith. I started with faith for a church of one thousand, then two thousand, then ten thousand. Now I have faith for a half a million."

He did everything he said. He had a "Yes, I can" spirit. He understood the promises of God and never stopped holding on, believing, until he obtained each promise.

When we got in the car to go home, my friends said, "We drove four hours and he was boring." One of them said, "I couldn't even understand him." But I caught the man's spirit. For little Timmy Storey, there was no more "just hanging on," hoping I wouldn't do something wrong. I started flexing my faith muscles and stretching out to obtain the promises.

When God gives you a promise, He'll give you a plan, He'll show you His purpose, and then He'll make provision. He's taken me around the world fulfilling His purpose in my life, and He always makes a way.

I can't tell you what it feels like to preach hope in the inner cities and see guys drop their Colt 45s, get down on their knees, and let Jesus change their lives. It's exciting. When you know the hell you came from and then bring hope to someone else, you can't help but shout. So get ready: Out of this unsteady time will come many opportunities to shout, because God will fulfill the promise He has given you.

It all starts with staying steady holding on to God's promises in the middle of the unsteady time. When God gives you a promise, it is a God idea. There's a difference between a good idea and a God idea. Good ideas come from the minds of human beings. God ideas come from the mind of God. Good ideas *may* come to pass. God ideas *will* come to pass; there's no doubt about it.

A God idea often has a greater purpose than we can comprehend at the moment. For example, on one of Paul's missionary journeys, he wanted to go preach in Asia, but God said, "That's a good idea, but it's not My idea." (Acts 16:6-40.)

As Paul and Silas continued on their way, every city they tried to stop in, God said, "No. That's a good idea, but not My idea."

Then one night Paul had a vision of a man calling them to come to Macedonia. He knew it was a God idea. So they traveled to Philippi, the foremost city in Macedonia. After being there for several days, Paul met a woman named Lydia, a wealthy merchant in the import/export business. She was the first person to open her heart to the message Paul was teaching down by the river. She and her household all got baptized, and she invited Paul and Silas to come stay in her home. She started having meetings in her home to tell others about the Jesus who changed her life.

But even in the middle of a God idea, opposition arose. As Paul and Silas walked about the city, a servant girl who was demon-possessed kept harassing them. Finally, Paul decided enough was enough and cast the demon out of the girl. He was feeling good. Life was great, and he was singing, "I got a feelin' everything's gonna be all right!"

But life was about to take another unexpected turn. The servant girl's masters were angry because Paul had hit them in their pocketbook. They had been using this servant girl as a fortune-teller to earn lots of money. These guys were so mad that they dragged Paul and Silas before a judge and incited the crowd against them. The judge ordered Paul and Silas to be stripped and beaten. That wasn't a cool situation.

Now, who sent Paul to Philippi? It wasn't his mother-in-law! It was God! That's right. In the middle of a God idea, all hell can still come against you. Life isn't perfect just because you're following God's plan and purpose. In fact, that's when you have to hold on to the promise most tightly.

I was watching the David Letterman show, and one segment of the show was about pet tricks. They brought a big tree into the studio, and a pit bull jumped up and ripped the limbs off, one at a time. Then he got to one big branch that he couldn't rip off, but he wouldn't let go. His jaws were locked. He growled and ripped and tore at that branch. The audience went wild. That dog would not let go of that branch until he pried it loose. That's how you need to be in reaching for your promise. You need to latch on and not let go, no matter what comes against you.

With Paul and Silas, things went from bad to worse. Not only were they beaten until their backs were raw meat, but they were chained to a wall in the inner prison with big rats running everywhere. Their feet were in stocks, stretching them to the point of breaking their pelvic bones. This wasn't a pretty sight.

But watch Paul's response. He didn't cuss God out or fax the other disciples and say, "It's just not worth it, this business of serving God." No, he and Silas responded by praying and singing praise songs to God while the other prisoners listened. Let's get real. Most of us wouldn't react that way. More than likely we'd be saying, "God, I must have missed You on this one. Get me out of here!"

You can really tell what people are all about when they're pressed. What's inside of them will come out. Paul and Silas were pressed, and they just kept praising and singing: "It's still gonna work."

I like what the great preacher E. V. Hill says about this episode with Paul and Silas in the prison: "I believe the angels were enjoying the song and stomping their feet to the beat and it caused an earthquake." That's right: When midnight came, *suddenly* an earthquake shook the whole prison.

God always shows up. He will never leave you when you're in the middle of a God idea, holding on to the promise. He does things *suddenly*. That's His style. *Suddenly* chains come off. It can happen if you'll keep on keeping on and ride out the storm. All storms die out eventually. Unsteady times eventually settle down. God will not take you through things you cannot handle. He's given you His power, so just stay steady and keep believing in His promises, as Paul and Silas did—and watch what happens to everyone around you when you do.

When the earthquake hit the jail where Paul and Silas were chained, all the doors in the prison opened and everyone's chains fell off. Paul and Silas were the ones who praised God, but their response in the middle of their trial didn't just loose them; it loosed everybody around them.

The best part of Paul and Silas' prison experience was yet to come, though it didn't look good at first. The jailer woke up, saw all the prison doors open, and assumed the prisoners had all fled. He drew his sword and was going to kill himself rather than face death at the hands of his superiors, because in Roman times if a prisoner escaped the jailer was punished and killed by methods that weren't pretty.

Now watch this. Even though it doesn't seem like it at the time, a lot of the trash we go through has a reason behind it. The chains come off, and here comes the reason for the prison experience.

The jailer was about to kill himself when Paul called out, "Time out, man. Don't get bloody here."

Don't you know that jailer was nearly scared stiff? He didn't think anyone was left in the prison. He called for a light, ran in, and fell down trembling before Paul and Silas. Then he brought them out of their cell and asked, "What must I do to be saved?"

Paul said, "Believe in the Lord Jesus, and you will be saved—you and your household." The jailer and his entire householdwere saved and baptized that very night.

So you see, the entire prison experience was a divine setup. Scholars believe the jailer was the first pastor of the Philippian church. He went to Lydia's Bible study, was taught by Luke the physician, and then was given the church. Sometimes you find the greatest gems after the most difficult expeditions.

God will lead you into places that are divine setups. Right now in the middle of this unsteady time in your life, it may not feel good—but God sees the whole picture. It's not just about the present; it's about the future. Paul later wrote a letter to the believers in Philippi that became the book of Philippians, the greatest motivational book in the Bible. He would never have written that letter to Philippi if he hadn't gone to Philippi in the first place. It was a God idea.

God wants you to live by His design, not by default. He has a purpose, an assignment, an agenda, an incredible plan for your life. Have you ever heard the saying "If you can figure it out, it's not God"? God doesn't do things our way or in our time, because He wants us to trust Him totally, to stop leaning on our own abilities and understanding, and to acknowledge Him in our lives. Then He will direct our path and make it smooth sailing. That doesn't mean we won't ever encounter obstacles, because we will, but He has given us the tools to sail right over them.

When you hold on to God's promises with a "Yes, I can" spirit, you're not going to cower down, back down, give up, or cry the blues when unsteady times come. You will join with the angels and sing and stomp your feet till the earth quakes and breaks the chains that have bound you and everyone around you. You will know that no matter how much hell tries to come against you in the middle of your God idea, God will fulfill everything He has promised you.

Chapter 3

⟳⟳○⟳

Battle Techniques

As you're looking to the fulfillment of your promise, understand this: You will have to fight for the victory, and the battle is always fiercest just before the breakthrough. Right before your victory, you may feel like all hell has broken loose. Don't give up too soon. Stay steady holding on to God's promises, and get ready to fight for them.

You need to get a new fight in your spirit. Be determined to not live a mediocre life. Believe all of the promises of God are yes and will come to pass in your life. Fight for the great life the Bible promises you.

In the middle of all the craziness in this world, you have to focus on the victory. In this battle for your breakthrough, you can't get distracted by what other people are going through or what anyone else is saying about your life.

Have you ever seen a horse in a race wearing blinders on both eyes? That's so he won't get distracted by the horses on either side. He focuses on the race and getting across the finish line. If you keep your focus on the finish line, your success, you won't be made unsteady by anything going on around you.

The battle will still rage against you, but there are several things you can do to stay steady. You can and you will win this fight to stay steady in unsteady times when you use these battle techniques.

First, start affirming people in a bigger way. Do you remember when you were little and didn't have much on your mind? You'd splash in puddles instead of walking around them. There in that very situation you don't like, why don't you go ahead and splash through some of the puddles of life and make big waves? Help somebody, inspire somebody, and change somebody's life. When you're feeling down, start saying something positive to somebody. Speak big. Stir somebody up. Speak life into people; shove it inside of them.

You reap what you sow. What you make happen for someone else, God will make happen for you. You may be saying, "Tim, you don't understand the hell I'm going through. I can't help anybody." But there is always someone worse off than you. There is still hope, and God is big enough to change your life and theirs, too.

Second, press the battle. In other words, be aggressive and run toward the battle. Did you ever wonder why all battle armor was worn on the front of the body? It's because you can't win a battle running away. As young David ran toward Goliath, you have to run toward the giant, not away from it. Stay on the offensive rather than the defensive.

Third, dream bigger. If the enemy has backed you into a corner, dream your way out of it. Activate your dream machine and think big again. If one dream dies, believe for a bigger one. When circumstances seem impossible, believe bigger, reach higher, and set new goals.

Some of your greatest dreams can come out of unsteady times. Out of all the discouragements and cheap shots I experienced, I saw myself touching Washington, D.C. I saw myself impacting celebrities and professional athletes. I dreamed bigger than even I could imagine.

In the middle of this battle, God is challenging you to dream and do big things. Some of the greatest songs and the most powerful books came out of desperate times. Sometimes it takes a time in the pit before we finally look up and see God is there for us. We try to get out, but we can't move forward or back or from side to side. The only way out is up, and that's where we bump right into God and all that He is: Provider, Healer, Good Shepherd, More Than Enough.

Let Him stir your heart with new dreams. It's never too late to start again. Taste the now of today. It's the future you've talked about in all of your yesterdays. What are you going to do with it? Set your imagination in motion, and stop looking back. After all, God doesn't consult your past to determine your future.

Fourth, pray bigger, harder, and stronger. Get out of your depression for five minutes and pray intense prayers. Put pictures of your family members in front of you and pray over them. Pray the kind of enough-is-enough prayers that will move the mountains out of their lives. Refuse to cower or be unsteady anymore. These days are intense, and the battle is fierce. You can't allow yourself to be lulled into a false sense of security. You have to be aggressive. Charge forward with everything you've got, and you'll discover that persistence will break the resistance.

Fifth, start speaking the promise. You can change your environment by speaking God's truth. Stop talking about the problem, and start talking about the victory. Life and death are in the power of the tongue. I like to say it this way: "You'll never reach the palace by talking like a peasant." Get your mind off what you don't have and onto what you do have.

Feast on God's promises. The Bible is filled with hundreds of promises that belong to all generations and apply to every aspect of life—faithfulness, hope, joy, happiness, talents, giftings, success, marriage, family, protection, security, promotion, guidance, knowledge, and wisdom—the list goes on and on. These promises are available to all who live according to God's principles.

I believe God also has specific promises for you that relate directly to His purpose for your life—financial security, good health, a godly spouse, restored family relationships, a child. Whatever your purpose, your dream, your vision, there is a promise to meet your need in fulfilling it. So embrace it as yours, even when you can't yet see any evidence of it in your life.

Sometimes all you have is a promise. Don't be discouraged when the circumstances don't add up to the promise. Be nourished and encouraged by it. Hold on to it. God will not lie. When you believe what *God* says about your situation, you will begin to change what *you* say about it. Believe that God can do what He said He would do.

God is big. Fill your insides with Him, and you'll start talking and believing like Him: *big*. "Man, I've been through hell, but I'm going to get a breakthrough." "I should have gotten that job, but I'm going to get the next one." "I don't know why that knucklehead left me, but God has someone better for me." It takes effort, but it's worth it when you see the promise becoming your reality.

Seventh, link yourself to a world shaker, a history maker, and a risk taker. If you don't know how to believe what you can't see with your natural eyes, then get around somebody who dares to believe the impossible and has the courage to see the invisible.

Stick with people who will keep telling you, "Everything's going to be all right." Their faith and positive belief system will get inside of you. Fill your tank with the right kind of fuel. Plug in to people who will wake you up, stir you up, help you up, and shake you up. Find people who have life inside them—life that will keep you moving forward.

Finally, in the middle of opposition and limitations, keep moving forward. God has put all of His power at your disposal, and you have a right to use that power not only to get through any and every battle you face, but to continue moving forward. You also have an obligation to clear the way for future generations. It's your responsibility to leave a legacy of faith.

Begin to forge that legacy by discovering the promises that God has given you in His Word. As you learn about His benefits, refuse to let them go no matter how heated the battle gets.

Learn how to believe God's Word even when you can't see it with your own eyes. His Word is the truth, and that truth can change all the facts.

Don't pause along the way to recount past failures, to indulge in self-pity, or to yield to negative talk. Stay focused on your journey. Remember: The key is progress.

You aren't the first to fight this battle, and you aren't alone. God is with you to refresh and revitalize you. He will give you a vision for a future that is better than anything you've yet dreamed. Allow Him to strengthen you and guide you into the victory He has already prepared.

If it seems as though you're stuck in a holding pattern in life, remember that God's purpose for your life is linked to His perfect timing. It is critical that you march on spiritually, receiving the revelation of His purpose, believe it with conviction, and follow His battle plan.

Don't fight against the plan of God. Too many times we want to live by default, rather than by design. There is a purpose for your life.

Life without a purpose is just an experiment. If you don't live by God's purpose, you will always be looking for the end of the rainbow, saying, "When I get such and such, then I'll be happy."

You can be happy right now on your way to the promise. Even if there are battles to win along the way, you should have a peace and a rhythm to your life because you're in the middle of a God idea. Right there, you can say, "This is God's idea, God's plan, and God's fight, and He already won—so I win!"

Chapter 4

❧

A Paved Pathway

When God has a plan, He knows the end from the beginning. God knew you would face the situation you're in right now, and He knows how it will be resolved. Often there is more to the story than meets the eye, and He needs you to follow His instructions to the letter. It may be a matter of life and death.

It certainly proved to be so in the story found in Acts about Ananias and Saul. When Saul (who later became the apostle Paul) was blinded on the road to Damascus, he knew he'd encountered the living God. (Acts 9.) Saul was well known for his zealousness in tracking down Christians—both men and women—and having them killed. He was feared in the

Christian community. So Ananias was flabber-gasted when God told him to go pray for Saul.

To Ananias it made no sense to endanger himself by going to find Saul. He had heard what sort of man this was. Here Ananias was about eighty years of age in his retirement years. He was relaxed in life, probably playing golf twice a week. Then along came God with this tough assignment. Imagine what was going on in his mind. He probably said, "It's bad enough, You disturbing me at my age for such a job, and now You're giving a murderer visions of me!" And being as human as you or I, Ananias tried to talk God out of it! But God knew the rest of the story, and He demanded obedience.

You see, God had a plan for Saul that was greater than anyone could imagine. He knew that as zealous as Saul was in his beliefs, he would be a mighty servant for His kingdom. Saul was a man who could not be compromised.

God also had a plan for Ananias, and it was critical that he obey and do exactly what he was told no matter how dangerous it appeared to be. Who could've ever imagined the impact Saul of Tarsus would have on generations to come? If Ananias hadn't been obedient, thirteen books of the Bible might never have been written.

You need to understand what it was like for Ananias because God may require the same from you. You'll be going along minding your own business, and suddenly God will do something big in your life. It may not make any sense, and it may even seem dangerous. But if it's a God idea, it's going to happen, so prepare for the unexpected because it's coming.

Just think how you would respond if I said to you, "Last week I led Charles Manson to the Lord, and he was baptized. I know he's done some bad things, but he's a changed man. They've let him out of prison, and he's out in the car. He needs a place to stay for a few days. Could you put him up in your guest room?" You would probably wonder, "Is this for real? Surely

God wouldn't want me to endanger my home and family by taking in a convicted murderer."

The point is that God's ways are not our ways, and He has an imagination that outdoes even Steven Spielberg's. You can't imagine what God has been dreaming up for you to do in these critical days ahead. That's why you're going through this time of transition right now.

From the beginning of time, the Lord has been saying to His people, "Get yourself in shape, deal with your character, attack the little foxes that spoil the vine." He wants us to take care of the little things that would hinder us, so we can make room for the big assignments He has for us.

He is ready to give you a God idea, to give you a purpose. It's up to you to be prepared to carry it out, so you've got to stay steady from transition to transition. Change is guaranteed. The pathway you have walked in the past may be very different from where you will walk in the future, so be prepared for God to stretch you and expand your horizons.

Rest assured that He has already paved the pathway of your assignment. He just needs your cooperation. Just as He paved the way for Ananias by giving Saul a dream that he would come and pray for him, He will pave the way for His plan for you. When unsteady times come, He will smooth out the problems and difficult areas in your life. Even as you read this, Jesus is personally praying for you—making intercession for you at the right hand of the Father. (Hebrews 7:25.) Warring angels are doing battle for you in the heavenlies.

So a pathway has already been smoothed. Are you ready to walk down it? Many people won't do it because they're caught up in their own routine. They're in a rut. How many times have you heard someone say, "This is the way I've always done it"? God is looking for people who will think differently, who are willing to break the mold and start over.

Breaking the mold and starting over, or going through transition, makes life seem unsteady.

That's because transition doesn't allow us to remain the same: We're forced to move. I view transition as a passage from one level to another. Once you pass through it, you can never go back to being the same. Once you're changed, you can never be exactly as you were before. It's like the old saying, "Once you've touched the fire, you can't live in the smoke!" Once you move into what God has prepared for you, you can't run back to normalcy. There's a "got to move" attitude drawing, stretching, pulling, kicking you. You're in transition, and you can't stay the same.

God uses times of transition to prepare ordinary people like you and me to do BIG things that don't make sense. For example, He asked Mary, an innocent young woman who had never slept with a man, to birth the Son of Man (Luke 1:26-37). He said, "I need a virgin to have My Son; and, Mary, once you move into this transition, you can never go back." Her words of faith, "Be it unto me," changed her life and the world forever.

God is looking for people who are willing to go from glory to glory no matter what the cost, because with every promise there is always a price. This time of transition that you are currently facing may feel unsteady, but it will lead to someone else's breakthrough. Don't try to force your own way out of it; instead, call on God to be with you right where you are and to pull you out.

When my daughter, Chloe, wanted to get out of her crib, she would start throwing things out onto the floor. Then she would start shaking the rails. If that didn't work, even though she could barely talk, she would scream, *"Get me outta heeere!"* Parents, you know how it is when you're trying to get a little one to go to sleep; you think if you just leave her be for awhile, she'll go to sleep. Well, it really shocked us when she learned a few more words and one night, shaking the crib rails with all her might, she hollered, "Get me outta heeere! I know you can

hear meeeeee. Ahhhhhhhh!" At last she had
found something that really worked!

Maybe you feel like Chloe did back then. In
the middle of this unsteady time, you may be
screaming, "Get me out of here!" But take a
moment to stop struggling against the situation
you're in and ask yourself a few questions: *Am I
fighting to hold on to a God-given promise, or am I
just fighting to get my way? Do I want out of this situation because it's unscriptural, or do I want out
merely because it's uncomfortable? Am I truly
seeking God's will and way?* Take some time to
uncover your real motivation.

You may be surprised to discover that you're
bucking against God Himself. The path He has
prepared for you may be far different from the
way you want to go. Although it may not be the
most convenient or the most comfortable, it is
the best. The key is your willingness to obey
Him. Obedience will help you find and begin
your journey on the paved pathway toward
God's promise of victory.

Chapter 5

∽○∽

It's Still Going to be All Right

One day I was taking my children to a movie and my daughter said, "I'm not even going in unless this one has a happy ending. The last one you took me to didn't have a happy ending. This one better have a happy ending." That's how we are in life. We want to know something is going to have a happy ending. Am I going to meet my goals? Am I ever going to fulfill my God ideas? Will my marriage break out of this rut? Will I lose this weight? Will I ever pay off these debts?

Jesus is the author and the finisher of our faith (Hebrews 12:2) and, yes, the story of your life is going to have a happy ending. Even if life is more unsteady than it's ever been, you have a promise: It's still going to be all right. You may be saying, "Right now I don't feel too good." It doesn't matter, because Jesus is personally going to walk with you to your victory.

When you're in an unsteady time, the enemy doesn't want you to have hope. He tries to bring discouragement and despair to keep you in the cement of hopelessness. But hope in Jesus, the author and finisher of your faith, will see you through.

If a dream dies, there is a grieving process, but you don't have to stay in the grieving posture. Did you know God gives life to dead things? Romans 4:17 NIV says, "God...gives life to the dead and calls things that are not as though they were."

Just look at Lazarus, Jesus' fourth-day miracle. He was part of Jesus' inner circle of friends, but he became deathly sick while Jesus was in another city having a healing meeting. When Lazarus' sisters, Mary and Martha, sent for Him to come immediately, Jesus spoke these important words: "This sickness will not end in death." It was a promise. When God speaks, He does not lie. He watches over His Word to perform it.

So when Jesus said the sickness would not end in death, everyone believed Him. His promise produced hope. Hope is the light at the end of the tunnel. Hope lifts your spirit when you feel discouraged. Hope helps you keep going when you feel like quitting.

Do you remember the level of hope you could feel as a kid? I remember one day when I was about eight years old, my daddy came home and said, "We're going to Disneyland on Thursday." I was so excited about going to see Mickey Mouse that I dug out my old Mickey Mouse ears from three years earlier. I had to use bobby pins to keep them on top of my big Afro. It was only Tuesday, but I wore those ears and barely slept for two nights waiting for Thursday morning to arrive. My daddy had made a promise, and my hope and expectations were sky high.

When Jesus said Lazarus' sickness would not end in death, their hope and expectation had to have been even higher than mine were for seeing Mickey! Mary and Martha must've been singing, "I got a feeling everything's gonna be all right!"

But Jesus took His time and stayed to finish up His healing meetings. You know, the disciples were concerned and one of them probably said, "Hey! Did Mary or Martha e-mail or call you about how Lazarus is doing?"

Jesus said, "Everything's all right. Our friend Lazarus is sleeping. I'm going to wake him up." The disciples were thinking, "Great! He must be doing better." They didn't get it. Then Jesus told them plainly, "Lazarus is dead."

It looked as if Jesus' promise had died. Lazarus had been dead and in the tomb for four days by the time Jesus and the disciples arrived there. Everyone was grieving and crying. But Jesus had a reason for waiting. The Jews believed that the spirit of a dead person hovered over the grave for three days and within that period of time, by some miracle, he might come back; after three days, they believed it was completely impossible.

They were saying, "Oh, man! That Lazarus has been dead so long, he stinks!" But isn't it just like God to wait until something is completely impossible in man's mind before He brings a breakthrough? Remember that old show-business saying "It ain't over till the fat lady sings"? With God, it's never too late!

Jesus was about to teach His friends, Mary and Martha and His disciples, who He was and what He could do. They were all used to seeing Jesus as the healer, as the One who gives peace and saves. But He was about to show them He is also the resurrection and the life. Just because a promise has died doesn't mean it's over, because He's the Lord over life and over death. They were about to see the resurrection power of God in action.

This situation required spiritual discernment. One of my preacher friends says, "You can't get an FM radio station on an am dial. When you're plugged in to the flesh, you can't understand the things of the spirit." The disciples and Mary and Martha didn't understand what Jesus was saying, because they weren't discerning spiritually. They were looking at the outward appearances and getting tripped up in the unsteady time. Jesus had said, "This sickness will not end in death." What He actually was saying in the Greek language was "The conclusion of this matter will not be death. When I am finished, he will not remain dead." Jesus never said Lazarus would not die; He said, "When I get through with him, he will not *remain* dead."

This was one of those situations where you have to jump the facts and get real. You may have a promise that appears to have died. You may grieve, but it's still not over. Remember: There is always opposition to a God idea. People may say, "Don't go there. The situation is so bad it stinks." They are the naysayers who look over your fence of life and say, "Well, I told you it was going to happen this way." Sometimes they are almost happy when it doesn't go the way you said it would go. Then they say, "Well, it could have happened if you hadn't done this." Or, "If you'd done it this way, maybe it would have worked out."

People may be talking behind your back and a TV news crew knocking on your door for an interview, but keep thanking God that He has already answered your prayers and prepared your victory. Don't let the enemy take away your loud voice, your shout, your joy, the skip in your step, or the glide in your stride. When your faith is in Him, you keep shouting, standing, walking, and staying steady.

Sometimes it doesn't look good in the natural, but remember: We walk by faith not by sight. When things look dead, God is maneuvering things in the supernatural for a resurrection. That's when your miracle is in motion. Don't worry about what it looks like; keep your eyes on Jesus.

If I could give you one clue to my success, I would say this: "I took care of the depth of my relationship with God, and He took care of the breadth of my success." Keep your focus on Him, because He'll make His promise good. When people begin to lose focus, they either run for a refuge—alcohol, drugs, cigarettes, food, a person, or a place to hide—or they run to THE REFUGE—Jesus! When trouble hits, where do you run? Examine your place of refuge, that place you seek in the middle of the storm, that place of significance.

David was often in trouble, hiding from King Saul or battling vicious enemies; but he found THE REFUGE. He wrote:

> God is our refuge and strength, an ever-present help in trouble.
>
> Psalm 46:1 NIV

> For You have been a shelter for me, a strong tower from the enemy. I will abide in Your tabernacle forever. I will trust in the shelter of Your wings.
>
> Psalm 61:3,4 NKJV

Sometimes we need a place of safety, a haven or place of rest, a secure environment to wait out the storm. I was in Florida a few years ago, and the weather station reported that a big hurricane was headed for shore. I was used to earthquakes, but I'd never been in a hurricane. Earthquakes are bad, but they just come unexpectedly and there isn't much you can do about it when one hits. But hurricanes keep haunting you and telling you, "I'm coming. I'm going to destroy you. I'm going to get you."

I called some friends of mine and said, "This hurricane isn't that bad, is it?"

"Oh, it's going to be a big one" was the reply.

"How bad?" I asked.

"Well, turn on the news."

What I saw on TV was enough to convince me to find shelter. Roofs were flying off and stuff was blowing all around. It looked like the movie *Twister,* minus the flying cows.

Life can be like a hurricane. Things can fly at you and go over your head, and you need a place of refuge. When you run to God, not only will He protect your physical body, but He will build you up on the inside. When you're built up on the inside, the things on the outside won't be able to shake you.

When David went out to meet Goliath, the giant, he was in THE REFUGE on holy ground; but his brothers were on the battleground and they were worn out. David was fresh and focused and had a great imagination. That's why David was able to knock a giant down with a little stone from a slingshot and then slay him with his own sword. David was in the place of refuge, in the Lord, and that was his strength.

The enemy uses circumstances, events, facts, and credible people to try to help the three giants of fear, doubt, and unbelief to defeat you. One more time they're going to shove that obstacle in Jesus' way, and one more time He's going to push it aside and say, "It's still going to be all right." He's calling your dream forth, and you're going to see it breathing new life again.

Chapter 6

Raise the Roof on Your Expectations

It's time to take the ceiling off and raise the roof on your expectations. Nothing is impossible for God; He's proved it over and over and over. He is in the miracle-working business. If God can make the heavens and the earth, part the Red Sea, and pave the streets of heaven with solid gold, He can take you to a higher level than you've dreamed—financially, physically, mentally, spiritually. Nothing is impossible for Him.

It's time to start thinking bigger and reaching higher. It's not good enough just to get through the struggles and setbacks. It's not good enough to barely get by each month. It's not good enough to have three good days out of seven. God has promised you bigger, higher things!

When God makes a promise, whatever He promises is guaranteed. It will certainly happen. In fact, the word *certainly* is mentioned in the Bible more than 1,200 times. When God speaks a promise, or a *certainly,* He means it's fixed; it's determined; it's settled; it's done. In street slang that means "Sure enough"; "I ain't teasing"; or "I ain't fronting." Certainly, God will supply all of your needs: He is the same yesterday, today, and forever. God is speaking *certainly's,* promises, God ideas, into you.

The enemy has tried to fight you in every way to stop you from getting God's *certainly's* into your spirit. It's one thing to get a certainly in your mind. It's another to get it deep down into your spirit. You will never move on something you don't truly believe in, but when it's in your spirit you will do great things. Say to yourself right now, "I'm going to get a *certainly* in my spirit!"

God spoke a *certainly* to Abraham in the Bible when He told this ninety-year-old man he was going to have a son. Abraham semi-believed as he was dialoging with God. But Sarah, his wife, heard what God was saying and laughed because it seemed so ridiculous.

The plan God has for you is so big that it will seem ridiculous to your mind. Abraham and Sarah's miracle was already in motion, and when they let that *certainly,* the promise of a son, drop deep down in their spirits, God gave them the desire of their hearts. God will do the same for you when you raise the roof on your expectations.

Like Abraham and Sarah, you will still find opposition to your *certainly's.* It's time to square up and face the facts. Become knowledgeable and understand the facts, but most importantly be honest with yourself. There is power in honesty. It is a fact that the opposition is there. It is a fact that desperate circumstances will arise, but God is going to give you breakthroughs and make a way to hurdle the facts when there seems to be no way. Plan on it.

Desperate circumstances trigger desperate, roof-raising faith. When you run out of rope, it's time to grab on to faith. Sometimes we have to get to the end of ourselves before God can mold us into the vessel of honor He desires us to be. He'll start by giving you the faith to jump one fact, and then you'll have faith to jump another and another. You'll find yourself saying, "It had to be God."

We can learn a great deal from a woman in the Bible who demonstrated desperate, roof-raising faith. She had been bleeding for more than twelve years and had exhausted her strength and finances seeking help from the medical community. No one could help her. She was considered unclean and untouchable according to the laws of her culture.

She was sick and tired of being sick and tired. She heard about Jesus and determined that if she could just touch the hem of His garment she would be healed. She wasn't going to strike out, blaming anyone else. She wasn't going to sit it out, never living a normal life. In her desperation, she reached out with desperate faith.

When the crowds were so overwhelming that it looked as though she'd never reach Jesus, she didn't stop. She did what she had to do. She dropped to her hands and knees and started crawling through the dust and dirt and donkey dung. All she could see were sandals and dirty feet, but she didn't give up. She kept saying, "I will live life again. I will be a wife to my husband again. I will be healed." Imagine how she felt when she saw the hem of Jesus' garment and reached out and touched it.

She didn't touch Him on His skin; she just touched His cloak—but He felt it, even in the middle of a crazy crowd. The Bible says Jesus was thronged by the crowd. That means there wasn't room to move. He said, "Hey! Who touched Me?" His disciples thought He had lost it because there were so many people touching Him.

But He said, "It was a different kind of touch." It was a touch of desperation and faith.

Jesus turned and said, "Woman, your faith has made you whole."

Like this woman, you can raise the roof on your expectations and say, "I'm not going to live like this. I'm not going to be down or depressed. If I have to crawl to Jesus, I'll do it. I'll get up one more time. I'll do whatever it takes to change my life to get where God wants me to be." God responds to desperate faith.

Don't you think Daniel felt pretty desperate when he was staring in the face of a dozen hungry lions that had been eating Christians for breakfast, lunch, and dinner? He had to raise the roof on his expectations, jump the facts, and believe God could shut the mouths of hungry lions so he could fulfill God's destiny in his life.

Daniel's story is probably one of the most famous in the Bible and has been told over and over for thousands of years to give people hope in desperate situations. God is the same God today as He was in the days of Daniel. If you'll respond to this unsteady time with desperate faith, He'll use your story to reach someone, too.

Even in the middle of this unsteady time, remember that God is at work. God has been doing some big things, but maybe you've been so busy trying to work through your struggles that you've missed them. You need to shift your dish.

I was at a friend's house to watch a football game. He lives out in the country and had just bought a new satellite dish. He was excited and couldn't wait to show it to me. He said, "Tim, watch this: wherever I shift the dish, that's what I pick up. I can watch games on the East Coast, in the Midwest, or anywhere."

It struck me. That is what we need to do. Wherever you shift your dish, that is what you will pick up. You can shift your dish toward "All things are miserable. Life is hard. I don't know if I'm going to make it." Or you can shift your dish to the All Things Are Possible Miracle Network. When you shift your dish toward God you get an expectancy mindset, which is vital in meeting your promise.

Sometimes in order to position you toward reaching the promise, God has to rearrange your life. When God called me into the healing ministry, I had never seen anybody healed. He said, "You're going to travel all around the world." At that time I hadn't traveled eighty miles away from home.

I needed to raise the roof on my expectations. God had to rearrange my surroundings and my friendships. It's like when you move into a new house: you have to find a new way to arrange the furniture. God had to bring people into my life who had a miracle mentality. Today I still purposely get around people who will stretch me.

God is stretching you right now. He has a plan for your life—and it's better than you've imagined. Maybe life has slapped you one too many times and you've lost your inner strength to dream. Not only have you taken a whipping on the outside but, as many of us do, you've been whipping yourself on the inside. It's a double whammy. You're bewildered and confused, just trying to hang on to survive. I can hear what you're saying: "I just hope I get a job to pay the rent." "I know he's not the best, but I guess he's good enough." It's not good enough to just pay the rent. It's not good enough to get someone who barely loves you. God wants you to have His best; don't settle for "good enough."

Maybe your life is full of so much trouble that you don't see how you could ever have God's best. But God will be your strength and deliver you out of all of your troubles. He stands close to those who are brokenhearted and wounded or crushed in their spirits from all the weight of dormant dreams.

> The righteous cry out, and the Lord hears them; he delivers them from all their troubles. The Lord is close to the brokenhearted and saves those who are crushed in spirit. A righteous man may have many troubles, but the Lord delivers him from them all.
>
> **Psalm 34:17-19** NIV

If you have lost focus on the Lord and His promise because you are overwhelmed by troubles or wounded in your heart, this word is for you. Hold it in your heart and let Him be your strength.

Remember how BIG God is. Stop thinking about how big your mountains are, and start telling your mountains how BIG God is. You're going to go through many troubles in life, but the key word here is *through*. You're not going to stay in them; you're not going to pitch a tent or build a Hilton Hotel in them; you're going to move on through to the other side, because God is going to deliver you out of them *all*.

So expect big things. You won't just get out of debt. Now you're going to lay up money for an inheritance for your children's children. No longer will blind eyes seeing be a hard case. No! You're going to start seeing as Jesus sees and causing others around you to be able to do the same. Even during this unsteady time, God is going to stretch you. You're going to learn to stand on His *certainly's*, walk on His *certainly's*, run on His *certainly's*, and soar on His *certainly's* as you raise the roof on your expectations.

Chapter 7

Get Ready for Victory!

Life starts out with a shout. Think about it. You came out of your mother's womb shouting. Babies learn to shout when they're hungry or wet or have a tummy-ache. Toddlers shout and laugh when they play together. Kids run up the steps, sling open the door, and shout to Mom when they run in the house after playing outside or when they come home from school bouncing off the walls, excited about life.

We start out living life with dreams, hopes, and expectations. Did you know there's a difference between living life and going through life? Living life means you have a skip in your step, a glide in your stride. You feel good, like when you were a kid and had the energy to chase down the ice cream truck, fly a kite, or ride a bike. You smile just because. That's living life.

But most people just go through life. They live by default instead of by design. Their shout becomes a whisper, and their step has a hitch in it. They start feeling the pull of unsteady times as their lives get shaken once, then twice, then countless times. Discouragement sets in. They start things but can't seem to muster up enough energy to complete them.

But it's not how you start; it's how you finish that's important. In a war there are casualties and injuries, some of which aren't even obvious until you stop to rest. Many of us need to be healed and restored in areas that have been torn or broken during unsteady times. When you're too fatigued and discouraged to finish the task before you, the Bible calls that having slack hands. When you can't shake this spirit of slackness (discouragement), it can be passed from generation to generation. Family members see this pattern repeated and begin to think, "This is just the way we live." But I believe a new generation is rising up that doesn't have to walk in slackness but rather can walk in victory, living life instead of just going through it.

You may be saying, "Oh, if you knew the hell I've gotten myself in. It'll take me seven years to get myself out of this mess." That's probably true—if you try to do it by yourself. But did you know that God's "super" on your "natural" will give you the ability to do things you can't do? Now I'm talking about the One with a higher power than yours: the King of kings, the Lord of lords, the Alpha and the Omega, the Beginning and the End, the Bright and Morning Star.

He is already shifting you. If you could just see in the spirit realm, you'd see the big old angels fighting for you right now. Big, bad, gladiator angels—standing there saying to your enemy, "Don't even think about it!"

I got an idea of what these angels could do when I was in Nigeria, Africa. The people around me seemed to be getting nervous, so I asked, "What's the problem?"

One of the men answered, "It's the witch doctors—they say they're going to kill you."

I felt like Dorothy in the Wizard of Oz: I wanted to go back to Kansas! Who wants to die in a place like that? I went into the meeting to preach, and these witch doctors were outside. I was preaching, and one of the guys on staff started screaming. I didn't know what was going on, but when I finished my message and walked out, he said to me, "I saw them! I saw them!"

I said, "Saw who?"

He said, "I saw your angels."

Seven different people came up and said they saw big, bad, gladiator angels holding hands surrounding me. That's what takes place in the spirit realm on our behalf. So stop worrying about winning a battle that has already been won.

If you have been feeling like you're fighting a battle because you've done something wrong, it's time to repent (if you haven't yet) and then get rid of your shame-based mentality. In the story of the prodigal son, the son went back to his father, dragging all the shame and disgrace along with him, prepared to beg for a menial job. This young man expected his father to show him a record of all his wrongs. He would have counted himself lucky to get a halfway embrace.

But the father had a restoration mentality from the very beginning. He fully embraced his son and brought him back into full authority as a son.

Like that dad, our heavenly Father extends His mercy and grace to us no matter how bad we act. He restores us to Himself when we repent and turn back to Him. God loves to party, and His victory parties are better than any Super Bowl party you've ever attended! Get ready for it.

Even now, in this unsteady time, blast through survival mode and into victory mode. Pulling up and out of your unsteady time is not just about survival; it's about overcoming because you are the head and not the tail, you are above and not beneath, and you are going over and not under. No weapon formed against you is going to prosper.

You need to believe this. Sometimes God allows us to get into certain situations and places to position us to learn how to hold on by faith, so you may go through a period of holding on. But a time of stretching out to pursue the dream God gave you must follow; otherwise, you will get stuck in survival mode. It's time to move into victory mode.

The quickest way to get into victory mode is to write down the promises God has given to you. If you haven't written down His promises, you won't be able to remember them when pressures come. Write them down and read them over and over so you will remember why God put you on this planet. It will put that pit bull fight into you when circumstances look the darkest and when people around you try to pry you from the promise.

The enemy is a liar and a thief, and he will send people to distract you and create circumstances to drag you down. He tries to pick your pockets and steal your dreams any way he can. He doesn't like you. So if he's been attacking you lately, don't take it personally: it's because of what you represent. You may become a millionaire who supports missionaries around the world. You may become the lawyer who prepares the case that throws out Roe vs. Wade. He hates what you represent.

You represent the One who promised, guaranteed, and won your victory, so get ready to obtain God's promises—no matter how tough it gets. My father died in a car accident when I was ten years old. My mother worked in Winchell's Donut Shop, not just one shift but two. She paid her tithes and gave offerings to several ministries believing God that somehow He would get her out of that situation. It was tough, but she never let her expectation level decrease.

She raised all four children in the things of God and taught us how to serve God. She stood on His promises and walked her talk when she said, "As for me and my house, we will serve the Lord." Three of us are now in full-time ministry slapping the enemy upside the head every chance we get. I thank God she never gave up. She didn't just survive; she overcame. God met her expectations.

While you're getting ready for your victory, it may not look like what God has promised will ever come to pass. Maybe you don't feel blessed right now. Maybe your bank account doesn't look blessed. Maybe when you try to write a check, the check bounces back. Maybe you looked at your family this Christmas and wanted to go on daytime TV to talk about it. But I'm telling you, you're still going to be an over-comer. You're still going to obtain the promises because all the promises of God are yes and so be it. When God says, "I will," you can bank on it: He will! So get ready for it!

That takes faith. The Bible speaks of five different levels of faith: weak faith, little faith, growing faith, strong faith, and great faith. Abraham did not have "weak faith." Even though his body was old and Sarah had been unable to bear children, he did not waver in his faith that God would do what He promised in giving him a son. (Hebrews 11:8-12.)

Jesus spoke to the disciples of their "little faith" when they awakened Him in the boat to calm the raging storm. (Matthew 8:26.) Paul wrote to the Thessalonians about their "growing faith." (2 Thessalonians 1:3.) Abraham had "strong faith" and was fully persuaded God was able to do what He promised. (Romans 4:21.) Jesus spoke of the centurion soldier's "great faith" when he asked Jesus to heal his servant. (Matthew 8:5-13.)

The faith you use to hold on during this unsteady time is the same faith you're going to use to stretch out and do everything God has called you to accomplish. It's just a different level of faith. Anyone who works out in a fitness center knows that building muscles requires persistent stretching and pushing to higher levels. That's exactly how you build your faith muscles.

When I started exercising my faith muscles, seeing myself preaching to ten thousand, then twenty, then thirty, and on up into the hundreds of thousands, I saw myself preaching all over the world, and everything I was seeing began to happen. At eighteen, I couldn't get into Oral Roberts University. At twenty-five, I was teaching there!

Do you catch the drift of what I am saying? I'm not sharing this with you to brag on what Tim Storey has done. I want you to realize this never could have happened with a "survival" or "just hang on" mentality. Holding on doesn't scare the enemy; it's when you stretch out that he gets nervous. People who stretch out have influence and impact—life-changing and life-saving impact.

You have to put out the effort it takes to be a champion and make this kind of impact. No matter how much ground you've lost or how far down you've gone, you have to leave the past behind and move toward the future.

Decide now to swing into victory mode. I love what my friend T. D. Jakes says: "You'd better get ready, get ready, get ready, because things are going to start sprouting, something's going to break out, someone's going to break through, a harvest is coming." That's the miracle-working God we serve!

Chapter 8

❦

God's Eye View

God has marked the path for your victory. At times that road may seem too steep, too slippery, or too long, but don't allow yourself to be overwhelmed by the journey. Your destination is not always a place, but often it's a new way of looking at things—through God's eyes.

You need to understand that you aren't fighting against flesh and blood but against rulers, authorities, powers, and spiritual forces in the heavenly realms. (Ephesians 6:12 NIV.) You have spiritual enemies whether you want to believe it or not. Just because you can't see them doesn't mean they aren't there. It was no different in Old Testament days when the king of Syria sent three thousand troops to chase down the prophet Elisha and his servant. (2 Kings 6:8-23.) Two against three thousand—that's how life feels sometimes. But watch the example God set before us in this story of Elisha and his servant versus three thousand trained, armed men.

Now, you've got to realize these Syrians are bad dudes. Nobody wants to mess with them. They cut off folks' arms and legs just to watch them suffer. They are sore losers, too. Elisha has been getting the Syrians' battle plans from the Lord and sharing them with the king of Israel. So this king of Syria is out for blood. He finds out where Elisha is and sends his army at night to surround the city.

When Elisha's servant wakes up in the morning, looks out the door, and sees the city surrounded by thousands of enemy troops, he runs in to Elisha in a panic and says, "Oh, my lord, what shall we do?"

Elisha says, "Don't be afraid. Those who are with us are more than those who are with them."

The servant replies, "But there are three thousand of them with chariots and spears, and they've got a totally mad look on their faces. Man, I told you we shouldn't have come against these people. Now they're out there with spears and ugly weapons. I don't see anybody else who's going to help us."

Elisha chuckles, "Hey, it's going to be all right. I'm telling you. Those who are with us are more than those who are with them."

The servant lets out a long sigh, "Okay, but you and me against three thousand doesn't make sense."

Elisha prays, "Oh, Lord, open his eyes that he might see." The young man's eyes open, and he sees the mountains full of horses and chariots of fire (angels) all around Elisha.

We have natural eyes, and we have supernatural eyes. We are so accustomed to looking with our natural eyes that we are blinded to the spirit realm. This is where we need to find a new way of looking at things. We need to see from God's eye view, through resurrected eyes. Don't let the fear of your circumstances blind you to God's supernatural solutions.

When you are feeling overwhelmed, don't fix your eyes on the obvious. Remember: God did not bring you this far to leave you. "The plans of the Lord stand firm forever" (Psalm 33:11 NIV). He is faithful to all His promises. If God gives you a God idea, He's not lying, He's not teasing, He's not fronting, because everything He says is "yes and amen."

Psalm 91:11 NIV says, "He will command his angels concerning you to guard you in all your ways." So right when you think you are all alone, God says angels have been commanded to guard you—not just one angel but hosts of angels, and not just in some of your ways but in *all* of your ways. When you consider all the stuff you've gone through, don't you think there was at least one angel working overtime on your behalf?

Elisha looked up to God and said, "I've got three thousand mean warriors and one scared servant—I need a miracle, God." God came through. Elisha had learned about God's miracles from his mentor, Elijah, who had fourteen miracles in a row. Did you know God even brings miracles in clusters? Maybe you haven't had one in a long time, so get ready for thirteen more. God can overwhelm you with miracles, to the point that you're saying, "Stop! It's too much!"

One day I came home with a bag of new video games for my son. He was so excited, and he said, "Dad, what'd you get?"

I said, "Oh, I think there's at least one blessing in this bag. Let me just see what I've got." But I already knew I had eight different games that a friend had given me. I just played it like maybe I had one and said, "Whoa, look at this!" and held it up.

Isaiah was jumping up and down and said, "Cool, that's just what I wanted."

I strung out the suspense and said, "Whoa! Look at this...and this...." The more I gave him, the more excited he got.

Finally, he said, "No, no, no, no." Then he jumped up and ran around the room in his pajamas and said, "That's too much; that's too much. Stop! That's too much!"

That's the way your heavenly Father wants to bless you—until you're saying, "Stop! I can't take the blessings anymore. I don't even know how to respond. I'm not used to being this blessed." You'd better learn how to become miracle-minded, how to get in the receiving mode.

Some of us have been plow-minded for too long. Here's what I mean. The law of the harvest says you plow the ground, you plant the seed, you water the seed, and you reap the harvest. Some of us have been so into plowing that we've forgotten we're going to get a harvest. There's a harvest breaking out here, and we're so busy over there plowing that we don't even see it.

We've got to learn to reach out our hands and be receivers. Did you know that when you refuse to receive a blessing from someone, you are blocking their harvest? When you refuse the seed from their hand, they can't reap a harvest. Don't get plow-minded and forget the harvest, even if you're going through a lot of *stuff* right now.

Elijah had fourteen miracles in a row, but he still went through *stuff* just like you and me. Elisha saw Elijah under the tree complaining and wanting to commit suicide. (1 Kings 19.) He heard Elijah say to God, "I've had enough." And God said, "Hey, eat some food and sleep a while; you're going to be better in the morning." He saw when Jezebel and Ahab were after Elijah. Elisha saw his mentor when he wanted to give up, and he saw him reach one more time for a miracle.

Elisha learned from Elijah, and one day he was faced with a servant who came back with a bad report, saying, "Man, Elisha, I think this is the end, but we've had a good life. It was cool. We'll probably end up in the Bible. This is it, man. I'm serious. There's a lot of ugly, mad guys out there looking to kill us. It's totally over now."

That's when Elisha was able to say, "Go up one more time, dude." Then he said, "Now,

God, do me a favor, resurrect this young man's eyes so he can see the way I learned to see." God gave that servant a God's eye view, and he saw the hills full of horses and chariots of fire all around Elisha.

Like Elisha, you are learning to see from God's eye view and say, "Those who are with us are more than those who are with them" (2 Kings 6:16 NIV). In the middle of this unsteady time, you are learning to not look at the obvious, but to look through resurrected eyes. Now reach up for one more miracle, and watch God blaze a trail, shake the world, and make history through you—all because you were willing to look at this unsteady time from the steady perch of God's eye view.

Conclusion

~⧜~

The Eyes of a Warrior

Recently, I was invited to speak to the Crow Indians. Out of a nation of 10,000 approximately 1,000 men and women came to hear a minister speak on motivation and how God can change their lives. The gymnasium was packed, and people were standing everywhere. I spoke from my heart with a supernatural energy and enthusiasm.

The next day, I was immensely honored as they adopted me officially into the Crow nation. The ceremony was awesome, and I was touched beyond words. They gave me a big hat with feathers, and I wore a vest and real moccasins. They danced their tribal dances and sang Indian songs to the beat of their drums.

The most rewarding part of the ceremony was when they gave me my Indian name. I was wondering what it might be—maybe something like "running mouth"! But they gave me a really cool name: "Warring With Wisdom." A leader in the Crow nation said to me, "When you speak, it's like a warrior comes out of you. You speak like a man who has been through battles." I thought to myself, "How right you are."

You see, the wisdom I shared with them and the wisdom I have shared with you in this book didn't come out of living a perfect life. It came out of a life of losing a dad at the age of ten, losing a sister two years later, watching the destruction in my family from generations of alcoholism, living in poverty, dealing with seeds of anger and rebellion, being misunderstood and at times mocked for my beliefs; but choosing to get out, choosing to fight again, choosing to break through and bust out and stay steady in every unsteady time. I can truly say, "I am a warrior." I'm not just speaking a message; I'm living a message! There's a big difference.

The chief said to me at the end of the ceremony, "Tim, it's in your eyes. There's a warrior in your eyes. You war with wisdom like a true warrior who takes back the spoils without getting blood all over his garments."

As you march through the unsteady times in your life and war with the wisdom you have gained in reading and applying the life-changing principles in this book, you will earn the distinction of being a mighty warrior, a vessel of honor, a champion of faith. You can do it. It's time for your breakthrough, so don't faint. God has already prepared your victory, so run to the refuge now.

I don't know what has caused the unsteady time you are facing right now, but I invite you to cozy up to your Daddy God. It's like building a fire on a cold winter night, grabbing a nice warm quilt, curling up on the couch and saying to Him, "Okay, I admit it. I'm not doing too good right now, God. I need You to help me. I don't have any strength left, but I know You do."

That's when God shows up. The Bible says in Isaiah 40:31 NKJV, "Those who wait on the Lord shall renew their strength."

When you're in THE REFUGE, all of a sudden strength starts to hit you and you think, "Oh man, I feel good." You're sitting, you're standing, you're walking, and you're feeling again. You answer the phone with energy in your voice. Your face comes alive. You've got some juice inside of you again. Now you're running and you feel like running isn't good enough. Suddenly, He picks you up and you begin to soar, just like the rest of the verse in Isaiah 40:31 NKJV says: "They shall mount up with wings like eagles, they shall run and not be weary, they shall walk and not faint."

This freaks you out, but you keep soaring and you begin to enter into what the Bible says in 1 Corinthians 2:9 NIV: "No eye has seen, no ear has heard, no mind has conceived, what God has prepared for those who love [and trust] him." You're soaring and you think, "How did I get this job? How did I get into this relation-ship? How did I get this life and this joy? How did all this happen?" God picked you up in the middle of a pit and caused you to soar. Once you experience this kind of soaring, you won't ever want to become unsteady again, because success breeds success.

You may not be exactly where you want to be, but you can thank God you aren't where you used to be. You're growing and evolving into His masterpiece, winning the battles of life. And don't ever forget: your breakthrough story may be the life vest that saves someone else who is drowning in the middle of an unsteady time. As you let others see the warrior in your eyes, they will know their lives will not end in the death of their dreams, one step from a promise, never becoming who they're supposed to be. You can be the one to make a difference in their lives, to awaken their hope, to teach them how to dream again, to raise the roof on their expectations. Reach out and touch someone today. They will be changed and so will you, not by what you say but by what you are—God's masterpiece.

Prayer of Salvation

God loves you—no matter who you are, no matter what your past. God loves you so much that He gave His one and only begotten Son for you. The Bible tells us that "...whoever believes in him shall not perish but have eternal life" (John 3:16 NIV). Jesus laid down His life and rose again so that we could spend eternity with Him in heaven and experience His absolute best on earth. If you would like to receive Jesus into your life, say the following prayer out loud and mean it from your heart.

Heavenly Father, I come to You admitting that I am a sinner. Right now, I choose to turn away from sin, and I ask You to cleanse me of all unrighteousness. I believe that Your Son, Jesus, died on the cross to take away my sins. I also believe that He rose again from the dead so that I might be forgiven of my sins and made righteous through faith in Him. I call upon the name of Jesus Christ to be the Savior and Lord of my life. Jesus, I choose to follow You and ask that You fill me with the power of the Holy Spirit. I declare that right now I am a child of God. I am free from sin and full of the righteousness of God. I am saved in Jesus' name. Amen.

If you prayed this prayer to receive Jesus Christ as your Savior for the first time, please contact us on the web at www.harrisonhouse.com to receive a free book.

Or you may write to us at
Harrison House
P.O. Box 35035
Tulsa, Oklahoma 74153

*Please include your prayer requests
and comments when you write.*

About Tim Storey

Tim Storey is a dynamic, gifted, and unique man of God in touch with today's culture and generation. *Lee Iacocca* says, "Tim is an energetic young entrepreneur with tremendous leadership abilities. His presentation style and delivery are nothing short of delightful."

Known as a tremendously powerful inspirational speaker, he's in demand both nationally and internationally with the purpose of training people in the style of Jesus. Tim has been significantly influenced by such men as Oral Roberts, Smith Wigglesworth, and others who were used in the gifts of healing. Through the grace of God, Tim Storey is now one of the strong young leaders in this generation. He is the only person since Billy Graham ever to be invited to speak on spiritual matters before Congress.

He is highly respected among professional athletes and has worked extensively at team chapels and training camps, most recently with the Oakland Raiders, Miami Dolphin, and Green Bay Packers.

Storey's Hollywood Bible Study is also changing lives in the entertainment industry. Known to be the mover of the movers and shakers, Storey mentors many of the industry's top producers, directors, actors, and musicians.

Storey studied for three years at South Eastern College and holds a Bachelor of Arts Degree from former Southern California College, now called